Mach II

Starring
YOU

Richard Bliss Brooke

First edition published 2000
Second edition published 2001
Third edition published 2003
Fourth edition published 2004

ISBN # 0-9700399-0-5
Published by High Performance People, L.L.C.
1875 North Lakewood Drive
Coeur d'Alene, ID 83814
Telephone (888) 665-8484, Fax (888) 665-8485

Printed in the United States of America

10 9 8 7 6 5 4

CONTENTS

FORWARD

Maybe you are like I was, somewhere in between a little confused to completely in the dark about what I wanted to do with my life. And, if I did figure that out... how I was going to pull it off? I really wanted to be successful, to contribute, to be respected, to be secure, and to have financial freedom. But I didn't know how.

The rules for doing so didn't work for me. Good grades, college, a family business or career counseling. Instead, I was fortunate to hook up with some people who had powerful alternatives, and given my history, I was fortunate to finally listen to them...the results have been staggering.

I had to hear this information a lot of different ways before I heard it in a way that I got it. I expect that when you study the flow of these secrets, you will get it too. Then, all you have to do is hold on.

—Richard Brooke

This is the true joy in life, being used for a purpose recognized by yourself as a mighty one. That is being a force of nature instead of a feverish, selfish little clod of ailments and grievances, complaining that the world will not devote itself to making you happy.

I am of the opinion that my life belongs to the whole community and as long as I live, it is my privilege to do for it whatever I can.

I want to be thoroughly used up when I die, for the harder I work, the more I live. I rejoice in life for its own sake. Life is no "brief candle" to me. It is a sort of splendid torch which I have got hold of for the moment and I want to make it burn as brightly as possible before handing it on to future generations.

—George Bernard Shaw

This book is dedicated to
Kurt and Jeannie Robb—
in honor of their gift of life.

The original title of this book was "Mach II with your Hair on Fire". The purpose of the title was to indicate the pace and momentum one could attain using the techniques in this book. On this the fourth reprint and rewrite we changed the title to better reflect the process, although for those looking at it for the first time it may not make a lot of sense!

MY STORY

★ ★ ★ ★ ★

"The American Pioneers had to become successful entrepreneurs... the Indians would not hire them."

Richard Brooke

Richard and sister Debbe trail riding in Yosemite, California in 1961.

I grew up on a cattle ranch in Chowchilla, California. At the age of four, I stole a pair of sunglasses from Red's Market. When my mom asked me where I got them, I told her the truth. She made me take them back and apologize to Red. I was totally humiliated. I decided telling the truth was painful and not a smart thing to do.

In the fifth grade, a girl I liked sat with me at a movie. We held hands. The very next day, she "dumped me." I decided I wasn't good enough for the women I liked.

In the sixth grade, we moved from the ranch to the city. The cool guys (the ones all the girls liked) wore powder blue Levi's

cords. I was still wearing K-Mart jeans—the ones with the double-patched knees. I decided I was not cool. I asked my mom to buy me the Levi's. She said, "No," or "Not now." I decided I was not cool enough.

> ### My Core Beliefs About Me — Ergo My Personality
>
> Telling The Truth Is Painful
>
> I Am Not Good Enough
>
> I Am Not Cool

Just like millions of other kids my age, I formed a personality to cope with life as I perceived it. As a result of a few silly everyday circumstances, I created a belief system and a way of behaving to go along with my beliefs. It was hardly a winning personality; low self-esteem, driven to belong and be accepted—and, thanks to

those sunglasses, I was a compulsive liar. I could have decided lots of different things about those early events. Why I decided what I did, I have no idea. The point is, my creative childhood interpretations of those circumstances became the truth for me—a truth that could have lasted for the rest of my life.

Graduating high school (by cheating off Stan Callan's civics final), I started my professional career pumping gas at Pearson's Arco at the corner of G and Olive Streets in Merced, California. I also lived at the gas station—in my pickup camper with Chinook, my faithful, yet obnoxious, dog. Eventually (after I failed to lock the front door of the gas station two nights in a row), my ambition led me to Foster Farms, the largest poultry processing plant in the world. It was a union job that paid $3.05 an hour, complete with benefits,

···★···

seniority, vacation, and best of all—retirement. I jumped at the opportunity. My job was to cut the chickens into parts as they flew past me on the production line…millions of chickens…billions of chickens. That's what I did for 450 to 530 minutes a day. Production people live their lives in minutes.

Although I was a hard worker, ambitious, and intelligent, there were some aspects of my personality that held me back. I disliked most other people. I refused to let anyone I considered less competent than myself ever tell me what to do. I worked my way up to teaching people how to cut up chickens. But, it didn't take long for my dynamic personality to put me back in my place. I just told my boss, Wayne, that he should go to hell—and I said it in front of his boss, Mr. Hoyt. That's all it took to put me back on the line. Regardless, I loved the chicken plant and still love the people with whom I worked. At that time, I fully expected to spend the next forty years of my life working there, building seniority (POWER), vacation time (FUN), and clicking off the years to retirement (FREEDOM). I thought I was really cutting it—life, not chickens.

That was 1977.
I was 22.

Foster Farms chicken plant. 1977

The Rest of the Story

What you're about to read may sound arrogant. However, it's true and necessary to make the point.

I made my first million before the age of 30, advancing to the top sales-leader position in a $60 million Network Marketing organization made up of more than 250,000 sales people. At age 31, I became the Executive Vice President.

At age 33, I accepted the opportunity to "turn around" a Network Marketing company. This company, when I joined it, was in a death spiral and technically bankrupt. It was almost $1 million in debt with no cash, no assets and no credit. With the help of a tremendous staff and my partner, Randy Anderson, we turned this company into a role model for the Network Marketing industry.

In March 1992, at age 37, SUCCESS Magazine featured me

and our company on its cover. SUCCESS called us "Millionaire Makers" and did a feature article on how the people we work with and trained built "overnight empires." And they did—and still do…not overnight, but many of our top sales leaders have built businesses worth well over $1 million. Several have become multimillionaires. SUCCESS Magazine has featured our company three more times since then.

In 1993, Sterling & Stone Publishing asked me to co-author The New Entrepreneurs: Business Visionaries for the 21st Century.

In 1994, I was nominated Inc. Magazine's Entrepreneur of the Year.

In 1995, our company was seen on NBC's Dateline, ABC's 20/20 and CBS's Good Morning America.

In 1996, Working At Home Magazine co-featured me on their

cover about how to get rich working from home.

In 1998, I was inducted into the Network Marketing Industry's Hall of Fame.

I've been to every state in our country, at least twice, as well as twenty foreign countries. I've been the featured speaker for countless groups numbering in the hundreds, and several times, in the thousands. Although not every area of my life has been wonderful, my health is great, I love where I live and what I do and I am blessed with dozens of loyal and loving friends.

I hope by now you're asking: "What happened?"

Here's what happened...

I changed. I changed my thoughts. I changed the people I paid attention to. I changed my mind. I changed my habits. I changed my attitude. I changed my clothes. I changed my opinions about me and about you. I changed what I read, what I watched on television, and what I listened to. I changed those deep-rooted decisions about who I was and who I would become. It wasn't easy, but it was just as simple as the decisions I'd made early on. I just decided to be different and do different things and then I kept deciding those new decisions over and over and over again, until they caught hold. And then, all I did was hold on!

Change is possible for all of us. You may have heard lots of clichés about how we cannot change who we are...but just ask yourself...have you changed? What events or insights in your life have changed what you believe and how you act? This is a good place to list them. Think about people that have come and gone in your life, events—some joyous, some tragic. Think about wisdom you have gained. Have you changed? If you have, you can change even more. I suggest that if it is on purpose and by design, you and I can change more in the next year than we have our whole lives. And in the next ten years, we can become a wholly different person manifesting wholly different results.

> **Change is not only possible, it is inevitable. The only question is, who is going to design it? What has changed you?**
>
> 1.
>
> 2.
>
> 3.
>
> 4.
>
> 5.

In May 1977, while still working in the chicken plant, I was introduced to a financial and personal development opportunity by one of my friends, Steve Spaulding. The concept was called Network Marketing. The company was Worldwide Products, Inc. Ironically, Steve was the guy who got me the job at the chicken plant. I think he introduced me to this new opportunity because he felt sorry for me.

There were several of our other buddies getting involved: Dave and Dan Austin, and the magnificent Jack Acker, now deceased. They were all friends who lived in the small ranching town of Merced, California. Although great guys, they were all seasonal workers at the local Ragu Spaghetti Sauce cannery, and—having mostly avoided any higher education at all—weren't the most credible bunch of fellows to follow into a financial opportunity. We were told that if we followed

• • • ★ • • •

the company's plan, we could earn more than $60,000 per year—part time!

In 1977, the only people in the world who earned $60,000 per year were:

- Doctors or lawyers.
- Extremely well-educated professionals.
- People given a successful business by their parents.
- Those who inherited a lot of money.
- Those lucky enough to have powerful connections in landing a super job.

I knew this to be true.

I knew I wasn't any of those people, therefore...

I knew I would never earn $60,000 doing anything!

But boy did I ever want to earn $60,000, more than anything in the world! This posed a problem: I wanted something I didn't expect would ever happen. The leaders of this financial opportunity were prepared for me and my dilemma. Apparently, it was common. They conducted intense training courses designed to resolve the problem. Their star trainer was a man named Kurt Robb.

On August 3 and 4, 1977, we all—the guys and I and forty strangers—sat in the Ramada Inn in Bakersfield, California, and listened for hours as speaker after speaker jumped up and down, telling us that we really could earn $60,000 a year—no problem.

And then came Kurt Robb.

Kurt told us how he used to work for Ma Bell in an Oklahoma factory...that although he was content there, he wasn't achieving all he desired…and then, at the urging of his wife Jeannie, he quit and joined her in a Network Marketing venture….

He said he had the same problem we did—that he *wanted* something he *didn't believe* he could have. Jeannie believed he could achieve anything. But Kurt told us he didn't believe it. So, they struggled and struggled, trying anything they thought could break them out. Eventually, after applying what he was about to teach us, Kurt broke through his *self-imposed limitations* and became an extraordinary success. Kurt and Jeannie were now traveling the world, helping other people achieve their dreams, and having the time of their life doing it.

Jim Acker, Dave Austin, Steve Spaulding, Bill Lane, Richard Brooke, John Callahan on their first cruise to the Bahamas.

So we listened.

What we heard about was a system—a "specific, proven procedure," Kurt insisted—that would bring anyone anything they wanted. A simple system that had actually been used for thousands of years to support human beings in achieving their greatness.

As he laid out each step; what it was; how to use it and what result was sure to come, I saw something about succeeding that had never occurred to me before…that you and I can achieve just about ANYTHING we set out to achieve, and it has little or nothing to do with luck, education, money or connections. This was completely mind-blowing for me. It went against everything I knew to be true. So, I thought to myself: If this is true, why doesn't everyone know this?

Why isn't this a required course throughout our school years?

How could algebra (whatever that is) be more important than this?

One of the people Kurt studied with was Napoleon Hill. Dr. Hill authored one of the most important success books of all time. Commissioned to do so by steel magnate Andrew Carnegie, Napoleon Hill lived in the homes of 500 of the wealthiest self-made people in America. He interviewed each of them to determine the success principles they shared. From his work, Dr. Hill wrote the classic bestseller, *Think and Grow Rich*. In addition, he wrote a series of manuscripts called *The Science of Personal Achievement*.

Literally hundreds of "personal growth and development" books have been written using the principles from Hill's works. *Mach II Starring You* is just one more—it's my attempt at communicating this extraordinary concept in a way that helped me understand it.

Five years later, I began studying under Lou Tice, founder of the Pacific Institute in Seattle, Washington. Mr. Tice's teaching provided far greater insight into Dr. Hill's earlier work. Through Mr. Tice, I came to understand how to teach what I had been taught.

Although Napoleon Hill had already passed on, and Kurt Robb himself tragically died nine months after I met him, both men had dedicated their lives to showing others how to find freedom and success through those principles. And their work did not go unrewarded.

None of us ever went back to the cannery or the chicken plant.

Every one of our lives changed that weekend.

Jack Acker passionately pursued his dreams with us for about five years, impacting everyone he touched with his gifts of laughter, fun, and a wicked golf game. We lost Jack to cancer. Dan Austin used his experience as a stepping stone to a successful industrial film business—mostly filming brother Dave. Dave Austin and Steve Spaulding are masters in their trade today. Dave is one of the highest paid Network Marketers in the world and an independent distributor for health care products. Steve is one of the best motivational speakers and trainers in the industry. Both have contributed their gifts to tens of thousands of others. Something quite magical happened that day in Bakersfield. And I share these stories with you in the hope that you will open your mind to the possibilities these techniques offer you.

If five guys from a small town can break out, so can you.

It's no fluke that a group of minimum wage, lower-than-low self-esteem, directionless, high school buddies found their magic and power and learned how to turn it up full blast. *Mach II Starring You* is about you making the same powerful discovery.

Here's how…

Every worthwhile experience, lesson, and new idea I've ever had was the result of a relationship I had with another person. The greatest gift of life lies in the diversity of other people and our relationships with them.

Since that eventful day long ago, I have created the opportunity to study literally thousands of people engaged in the pursuit of their own success. These people have spanned every socioeconomic group, religion, race, occupation and geographic location imaginable. I have studied with some of the most popular success coaches of our time; from Lou Tice of the Pacific Institute to Tony Robbins of Robbins Research in La Jolla, California. I have listened to or read the works of most gurus, teachers, and masters in-between; including Stephen Covey, Spencer Johnson, Bob Proctor, Brian Tracy, Og Mandino, Richard Bach, Earl

Nightingale and Wayne Dyer, plus a host of radical and obscure teachers as well. My experiences working with these people, as well as my own success, have supported every aspect of this sure-fire system for success. This stuff works—and anyone who has succeeded "on purpose" has used it—knowingly or not.

My intention in writing this book is to contribute some ways of communicating these ideas that have helped me understand and implement them. I intend for this to be a quick-and-easy inspirational read. It should be reviewed and given to those you wish to support in their quest for success.

I have focused all that I have learned into one pivotal concept and procedure I call vision and self-motivation.

Without it, nothing else will work.

With it, nothing else matters.

At the pinnacle of his success, Kurt Robb was suddenly and tragically killed in the rugged surf of Hawaii. Jeannie was with him. It was their first success-spurred, "no expense spared" vacation.

Kurt's teachings had such a profound impact on my life that he instantly became one of the most important people in it. Then he left—for good.

While Kurt was alive and training me, I never implemented anything he taught me. I was "getting trained," "working on it," and "preparing." When I first heard of his death I reacted by quitting—feeling that without him always there to help me get ready, I couldn't go on. Hours after quitting, I realized that my reaction was a cowardly dishonoring of Kurt's gift, and that I could only honor his contribution by becoming, from that moment on, a source for others. No longer could I be "getting ready." I had to implement and teach others to do the same.

My life changed dramatically that day. That day, I committed to be the source for myself and others, to do what I knew could be done.

SUCCESS SECRET ONE:
SELF MOTIVATION

★ ★ ★ ★ ★

"You miss 100 percent of the shots you never take."

Wayne Gretsky

Don't Worry—Think Happy

This book is about motivation— Self-Motivation. It's about starring in, directing and producing the movie of your life—with powerful results. It's about taking your desires, hopes, dreams and aspirations and turning them into roaring fires of accomplishment. And, it is also about how to do this all by yourself...anywhere you want...anytime you choose... for the rest of your life!

having everything you want, comes APATHY. This book is simply about accelerating the momentum of your every success for the rest of your life! People are happiest when they are in the process of achieving... when they're accomplishing something that's tremendously important to them. It's the anticipation of getting the intended result...knowing you're on the right track... moving forward...in momentum... that makes you happiest.

So much of what the great athletes do to accomplish the impossible is done through visualization. Mach II captures exactly how it works; why it works; and how anyone can use it to do great things in their life.

John Elway—Super Bowl MVP

However, this book is NOT about achieving everything you've ever wanted. That's not a place you will ever want to get to—not that you ever could. For along with

Do you remember when you bought your first car? Do you remember how you felt in the weeks, days and hours leading up to the purchase...the period of time when

you knew you were going to get it, but you were still working on financing or delivery? Do you remember the high of anticipation? These feelings are the essence of my definition of success.

Do you remember the promise you made to yourself and others about how the car would never see rain, you would never eat in it, or abuse it in any way?

Yes…and then what happened after you got the car? Do you remember how the feelings slowly diminished? If you were like me, it only took a couple of weeks before you were driving through mud, eating a burger and fries and yes, back in those days, puffing away on a cigarette.

Achieving the result itself has such short-lived pleasure.

The essence of being truly alive comes with falling in love with the pursuit of your dreams…always stretching…always in momentum…always expecting the best.

This is Winning.
This is Success.
This is Living.
This is Happiness.
This is Mach II Starring You.
And SELF-MOTIVATION is your key.

The Four Great Lies of Success

1. Desire Creates Success

Most people confuse motivation with desire. We think because we want something bad enough we will have the energy to get it. Yet, how many people do you know who have a strong desire for a great deal more in their lives?

And…how many of them have had that desire for a long time?

How many are achieving it? The fact is, almost everyone has desires for health, wealth, and happiness— and almost no one achieves all three. How many people do you know who even have two?

A Social Security study conducted by the Bureau of Labor Statistics revealed that of 100 people who started working at age 25, by the age of 65…

- 63 were dependent on Social Security, friends, relatives or charity.
- 29 were dead.
- 3 were still working.
- 4 had accumulated adequate capital for retirement.
- 1 was wealthy

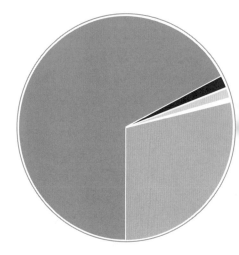

With forty years to plan and work for their future, only 5 percent—just five people—were financially successful!

Desire has absolutely NOTHING to do with motivation. Desire only creates the yearning for something but not any of the actual magical energy it takes to stay on the path towards it.

2. Hard Work Creates Success

Do you want to be successful? Then work hard! But haven't you been working hard? How many people do you know who have been working hard their whole life? If you worked twice as hard as you do now…if you worked twice as many hours every day… would you be successful? (Or would you be divorced and dead?) Does hard work necessarily have anything to do with success? I am not advocating not working hard. It just does not necessarily lead to you getting what you want. It is a great asset but not the answer we have been led to believe it is.

3. Being a Good Person Creates Success

Be a good person. I am not advocating anything else. But what does being a good person have to do with success? How many successful jerks do you know? Haven't you seen the evidence that "money has no conscience"? It doesn't care where it goes. Neither does health and in many domains of knowledge, neither does wisdom.

4. Getting a Good Education Will Lead to Your Success.

Again I am not advocating getting as good an education as you can.

Yet the world is filled with educated derelicts. Education does not insure anything. It confirms that we know how to study and pass tests. The age-old truth of getting great grades and getting into the best college is as good a strategy as working hard and being a good person. But it will not necessarily lead you to the good life.

THEN WHAT DOES LEAD ME TO GETTING WHAT I WANT IN LIFE?

The Secret to Success

If thousands of people have found the secret to success, then it's got to be Self-Motivation. Self-Motivation is that mysterious concoction of belief, confidence, positive expectations and creativity—a seeming abundance of physical, mental and emotional energy—that naturally propels us to our goals. Check it out for yourself.

If you could get yourself motivated enough...

And keep yourself motivated enough...

What do you think you could achieve?

Let's start out by defining Motivation.

Motivation is a powerful blend of physical, mental and emotional energy focused on creating an intended result.

Motivation is the energy which LEADS us TO ACT and causes us to ATTRACT:

Physical Energy
Courage
Enthusiasm
Persistence
Creativity

DIRECTOR'S NOTES

WHAT IS SUCCESS?

- Success is moving forward toward what you want, being in the process of achievement, and being in love with the process.

- Success is not getting everything you ever wanted.

- The first secret to success is Self-Motivation— that emotional, internal energy that leads us to act powerfully.

Look at each of these separately and ask yourself:

- If I could generate and sustain enough *Physical Energy*, could I accomplish what I want?

- If I could get and keep enough *Courage*, could I?

- If I could get and keep enough *Enthusiasm*...enough *Persistence*... enough *Creativity*, could I?

Let's take Creativity, for example—the most powerful form of motivation. The only thing standing between where you are now and where you want to be is a series of problems. Problems such as:

Not knowing how to do something...

Not having enough time...

Not having enough resources or support...

DIRECTOR'S NOTES

VISION CREATES SELF-MOTIVATION.

- To the degree there is a contrast between how we are performing now and how we envision ourselves performing, motivation pours forth.

- This is an automatic and natural effect. It flows whether we want it to or not.

Not having the money…

Not being able to get people to do what you want them to do…

All of these are examples of things that can prevent you from accomplishing what you want. We all have many examples of such problems. Solve these problems, and you break through to success.

Now, look back over your life to a time when you successfully achieved a goal you had. Think back a little bit further to just before you accomplished that particular goal. Notice the problems, obstacles and challenges you met and overcame along the way?

How did you do it? Obviously, you solved those problems, but where did those solutions come from? The solutions came about because of *ideas you had.* Ideas are the results of your creative thought. When you're motivated enough, you will come up with ideas…

new and different ways of doing things…a different way of saying things…even a brand new way of SEEING things.

Creativity is not the exclusive property of genius. Creative thought is the direct result of being MOTIVATED.

We *all* have the ability to generate creative thoughts whenever and wherever we want.

The same is true for physical energy, courage, enthusiasm and persistence. These energies and decision-making abilities are available to us on demand, in extraordinary quantities. Our emotional state and our state of mind determine when and how we unleash them. Take a moment to reflect on the times in your life when you have called on them and they were there.

·· ★ ··

These Are Your Successes.

YOU are an infinite storehouse
of *physical energy*.

YOU are an infinite storehouse
of *courage*.

YOU are an infinite storehouse
of *enthusiasm*.

YOU are an infinite storehouse
of *persistence*.

YOU are an infinite storehouse
of *creative genius*.

OF ELEPHANTS AND FLEAS

Have you ever wondered how the circus keeps a 4,500-pound elephant tied up with only a flimsy, little rope around one of its huge ankles?

Simple conditioning.

When the elephant is a little baby (weighing only a couple hundred pounds), they secure one of its hind legs with a heavy steel chain. Every time the elephant tries to wander off, the chain jerks the animal back. After a while the elephant's ankle gets raw and sore. If it continues to tug at the chain, it experiences more and more pain.

It doesn't take too long with this kind of conditioning for the elephant to decide that tugging equals pain.

Eventually, a simple strand of rope is all it takes to restrain the huge creature.

Fleas—as the positive mental attitude guru Zig Zigler has taught us—are trained in a similar fashion. The trainers put their fleas in glass jars and secure them with a cover on top. As the fleas try to jump out of the jar, they continuously bang their heads on the lid.

The flea trainer knows when his job is done because the fleas—expecting to be stopped by the lid—will jump no higher than the cap of the jar regardless of how much they want out. Then the lid can come off. The fleas have decided that jumping high is painful.

You and I are a lot like fleas.

REVIEWING THE SCRIPT

THE ONE THAT'S ALREADY IN PLACE

★ ★ ★ ★ ★

"Restlessness and discontent
are the first necessities of progress."

Thomas Edison

Whether You Know It Or Not...
Whether You Want It To Or Not...

Your heart beats 103,680 times a day.

You breathe 23,040 times a day.

You generate 3,000,000 nervous impulses a second.

Your stomach develops an acid strong enough to dissolve nails.

Your entire body runs on very small, electrically charged particles.

And all of this is happening whether you know it or not...whether you want it to or not...and, *you already have visions that motivate you to do what you are already doing.*

One of the primary unconscious functions of the human mind is releasing, on demand, sufficient levels of Self-Motivation. Your mind, through your vision, creates and produces enthusiasm, persistence, physical energy and, most importantly, creativity. This is a natural, ongoing process. You are either aware of this gargantuan power and manage it to produce your intended results, or you allow it to run rampant—amuck and aimless—usually at little more than idle speed, chasing its tail in a vicious circle of mediocrity. Don't ask me why about all of that; I'm in total wonderment. But the fact is, your mind does produce this effect for you. Your script is already in place—it's even self-monitoring.

The following statement communicates this as best I can:

To the degree that there is a contrast between what we have decided *should* be happening (visions) and what *is* happening

(current results), MOTIVATION naturally, effortlessly, powerfully and infinitely flows.

It does this instantly, as soon as it recognizes that a contrast exists.

The best analogy for how this works is a thermostat.

Let's say the actual temperature (what *is* happening/current results) is 65 degrees, and you set the thermostat at 70 degrees (what you've decided *should* be happening). There is a contrast between them. So, the thermostat signals the heater to produce heat (motivation) until the temperature hits 70 degrees; at which time the thermostat signals the heater to stop. The temperature in the room starts to cool back down almost immediately. When it drops below 70 degrees, motivation, in the form of heat, begins to flow and the warming-up process begins again. Back and forth, back and forth, the temperature rises and falls, constantly in

DIRECTOR'S NOTES

WHAT IS VISION?

- A vision (for the purposes of creating motivation) is the same as an expectation, a belief or a mindset.

- A vision is simply how we see ourselves; the conversation we have with ourselves and the way we feel about ourselves in any given endeavor.

HOW DO YOU CREATE A VISION?

Everybody has had, and will have, a vision. It is not a matter of getting one; it's a matter of replacing the one you have with the one that propels you toward your goal.

search of 70 degrees. (Thank you, Bob Proctor.)

So, too, when what *is* happening in your life contrasts with what you decide *should* be happening, the "thermostat" in your mind releases motivation to bring the two together to create alignment. As the two come together, motivation is momentarily reduced, only firing up again as they drift apart.

If there is no difference between what is going on and what you expect to be going on, you have no motivation.

There is nothing for your mind to pursue.

You have no need for physical energy, persistence or creativity.

You are, in a word, apathetic.

Some people call it lazy, others bored.

Lost souls in the sea of humanity.

Victims of their own mind crimes.

Lemmings leading themselves off the cliffs of resignation, despair... hopelessness.

Your mind doesn't care about what you want—or what you're willing to work hard for. It only cares that you perform in accordance with what you expect for yourself. If that requires an adjustment up or down, one step forward or two steps back, your mind doesn't mind. It's like a script that is already in place.

There are Three Basic Forms of Vision

Positive:
Your vision is aligned with your goals.

Neutral:
Your vision is not aligned with your goals, but rather is a reflection of your current results.

Negative:
Your vision is not aligned with your goals or your current results, but rather the results are even further away from where you want to be.

···★···

ON FIRE, APATHETIC, OR WORRIED?

| A positive vision will motivate you to achieve your goals. | A neutral vision will create apathy or only enough motivation to sustain the status quo. | A negative vision (worry) will actually motivate you to sabotage all current results. |

An article in the *Wall Street Journal* put it this way:

"The power of expectations in the classroom is downright scary. In a typical experiment, elementary school teachers were told that one group of kids had done extraordinarily well on a test that predicts intellectual 'blooming,' and so would make remarkable academic gains. The test seemed prescient: After a few months, the 'bloomer' it identified had achieved statistically significant gains over the other students. In reality, there was no such test. To the contrary: The kids the teachers thought were bloomers included students from every ability level. The only difference was in the mind and expectations of the teacher, yet those expectations produced clear academic differences."

Why Diets (and other things) Don't Work...

Motivation is not the only force that can lead you to action. It is the only thing that can sustain you. Sometimes your reality can

DIRECTOR'S NOTES

HOW DO YOU KNOW WHAT YOUR VISION IS?

Look at your actions. Your actions are always consistent with your visions. You are on the path to where you envisioned going.

be altered by force or by the impact the motivation of other people has on you.

For example, what happens if, through hard work, desire, circumstances, or just plain luck, you create a result that differs significantly from what you normally would expect. Let's say you've had a particularly good month in business and you earned twice as much money as you normally make. Or, perhaps you developed this burning desire to get back in shape physically, so you watched what you ate and worked out consistently for a whole month. You lost weight and looked great.

But then what happens?

You gain back the weight you lost—and then some!

Why?

Unless you quickly change your decision about you, your mind will unleash whatever subtle, yet

powerful motivation is needed to bring you right back in line with what you really thought would happen—even if those thoughts are not what you want.

In this example, although you did lose the weight and looked great, you were still expecting to be overweight. Sooner or later, you were destined to be back where you started—out of shape and overweight—simply because that's what you were motivated to do. Remember, this is all natural and automatic. It's instinctive. It does not matter what you want and work hard for. You get what you expect.

In sports, when this happens, it's called choking.

Here is how this system played out in my money-making efforts. When I started out in my new $60,000 a year Network Marketing opportunity, I started with a decision that I could not make that kind of money. I wanted

• • • ★ • • •

to make it. I hoped I could make it. I wished somehow I would get lucky. And, I didn't want anyone to know that I didn't think I could do it, so I tried.

I worked real hard; I invested everything I could get my hands on. I traveled everywhere, learned everything I could, and I made $12,000 my first year. Then I made another $12,000 my second year. (This is the same income I earned as a chicken cutter.)

Then I got tired of working so hard, so I took it a little easier and earned $4,000 my third year. You see, even though I wanted to earn $60,000 and I did everything I could think of to do it, I was working against an anchor dropped years earlier. A life-limiting decision like, "I wasn't good enough." (Remember the girl who dumped me in the fifth grade?) "I didn't need anybody." A bad position to be in when you're supposedly building a network of thousands.

So, finally, after losing everything I had, including my home, three cars (repossessed), and all my

DIRECTOR'S NOTES

Most people's visions are based solely on what they have been experiencing. Experience, for most of us, is "the truth," and we bind ourselves by that truth.

LLYWOOD
ODUCTION
RECTOR
AMERA
DATE   SCENE   TAKE

credit, I finally hit bottom and I woke up. You see, even though I had been taught what to do to succeed, "I didn't need anybody," including some of the greatest minds of our time. I "tried" to make myself succeed. I tried to force it without changing what I thought about me. In my desperation (faced with returning to the chicken plant a failure), I decided to implement what Kurt Robb had taught me three years earlier.

I went to work on my head—my thoughts—what I held to be true, literally changing my mind about what I had decided about me. It worked. Within six months, I was earning $10,000 per month—within two years I was earning almost $40,000 per month. Think about that: $4,000 a year to $400,000 within two years!

Richard Poe, in his book, *Wave 3: The New Era in Network Marketing*, suggests the reason for my positive change. He says that to succeed in MLM, you must become a positive thinker. Without a relentlessly positive outlook, you can neither see nor recruit. Your business will shrivel and die at the first onslaught of adversity.

Like the legendary UCLA basketball coach John Wooden, veteran networkers understand that success comes not from avoiding problems, but from dealing with each problem courageously. "Things turn out best," says Wooden, "for the people who make the best of the way things turn out."

I was a typical negative thinker. Although my parents were affluent, college-educated ranchers in California, my downbeat attitude made success in life a long shot. My parents divorced when I was 17. I hated school. I didn't study and skipped a lot of classes. I barely graduated with a D average, and so I didn't even try for college.

For a while I thought it might be nice to be a forest ranger. But then, a ranger told me that I would need to get a college degree first. Even then, the ranger warned, only 300 applicants were selected per year out of 3,000.

A nanosecond after he told me that, I decided that I couldn't be one of those 300. Of course, I was right. I couldn't, because I believed I couldn't.

Everything changed for me when I developed the willingness to train myself to think like a successful person.

Of course, most people lack the success thought process, initially. But I had an even worse problem. I lacked the willingness to acquire the success thought process. And that will stop anyone dead in their tracks.

The first time I was confronted with the science of motivation, I rebelled. In training sessions for a fuel additive company, my instructor urged me to write down my goals and to study motivational books like *Think and Grow Rich*, by Napoleon Hill.

"If you read this book," the instructor promised, "and read other books like it and listen to tapes by successful people, you will begin to think the way they do. And, once you start thinking those thoughts and believing those beliefs, you will become as successful as they are."

I thought it was baloney. My problem was that I "knew" that success had nothing to do with my thought process. Success came from getting straight As in college and having a Rolodex filled with influential connections. Everyone knew that. But, I read the book anyway.

At first, I hated *Think and Grow Rich*. It might as well have been written in Greek. I took over a year to slog through the slender volume, which many readers devour in a matter of days. The thoughts in this book were so contrary to my beliefs, I rejected them. That book and I were like repelling magnets, like water off a duck's back.

If only I knew what I was rejecting!

In the early years of this century, the legendary steel mogul Andrew Carnegie had imparted to Napoleon Hill—at the time, a struggling young journalist— what Carnegie believed to be the secret of his success. Hill then spent the next 20 years inter- viewing over 500 other wealthy and successful men, including Theodore Roosevelt and Thomas Edison, in order to gain their secrets. The results of his epic survey were revealed in Hill's classic books, *The Law of Success* (1928) and *Think and Grow Rich* (1937). Hill had discovered that all great achievers build their success around a single, simple principle, which alone had the power to transform a pauper into a billionaire. But, I didn't want to hear it. I thought I knew better.

I might have gone through my whole life rejecting this life-giving information. But, as so often happens, I was saved by a personal

DIRECTOR'S NOTES

THE LIFE CYCLE

Occasionally we get enough positive input about a change to expect the change to pay off. We fall into a new vision...motivation pours forth, and we leap into action, succeeding here and there.

crisis. Few things are more conducive to action than having your back to the wall. I found that out the hard way. My greatest despair led to my ultimate salvation.

For the first years of my Network Marketing business, I had relied for emotional support upon a man named Kurt Robb. Robb was the head sales trainer for my company and I idolized him. In training classes, I hung on Robb's every word, soaking up inspiration. When I was down, Robb would always pick me back up. I saw him as my hope and having him around was my security blanket.

Then, one day, Robb was killed. A freak wave hit him on the beach in Hawaii. His head struck a rock and he drowned. I was devastated.

I realized then that I had a choice. I could choose to quit because I'd lost my mentor. Or, I could honor him by taking what he'd taught me and implementing it.

Until that point, I saw myself as a permanent student. I had put off actually using Robb's techniques because I thought I still had more to learn. But now, my teacher was gone and there was no more excuse to wait. I decided if it's to be, it's up to me.

I set to work mapping out my goals—something Robb had told me to do years before. I started every day with a chapter of Napoleon Hill or a bracing dose of some other motivational book or tape. I read *As a Man Thinketh* by James Allen, *Psycho-Cybernetics* by Earl Nightingale, Og Mandino's *The Greatest Secret in the World*, *The Magic in Believing* by Claude Bristol and many more. All day long, I would repeat positive phrases to myself, programming my subconscious mind to expect success. At night, I closed my eyes and visualized myself closing sales, recruiting top performers into my downline, and raking in scads of cold, hard cash.

At times, I felt like an idiot. Was this really me? The perennial skeptic? The cynic? Was I really behaving like all those wacky "positive thinkers" I'd mocked and teased for so many years?

Yes I was. And in no time at all, my new regimen began to bear fruit—big fruit. I expressed my new philosophy by quoting Napoleon Hill:

"The world has the habit of making room for the man whose words and actions show that he knows where he is going."

I had learned the secret to success—that single, simple principle about which Napoleon Hill had written more than 50 years before. It was the power of goal setting.

Most people have goal setting confused with desire. People think that if you write down all the things that you desire, that's goal setting. It's not. Everyone is a goal setter and a goal achiever,

DIRECTOR'S NOTES

EXPERIENCE IS THE TRUTH.

And the truth is what we expect. Therefore, we tend to be motivated to only maintain the status quo.

whether consciously or not. Goal setting only works when your goal becomes your MIND SET OR EXPECTATION. If all you do is think of things you want and write them down your "wanter" will be working really good but your "getter" will still be asleep. Goals have to become beliefs and expectations. You have to believe what you want is actually inevitable.

In the early days, I expected to fail. That was my unconscious goal, and I "achieved" it again and again, much to my dismay.

When I tried to recruit someone into my downline, I'd say something like, "Gee, I don't know if you'd be interested, but maybe you'd like to hear about this part-time opportunity…."

Deep down inside, I didn't really believe that anybody in his right mind would sign up for my downline—and it showed. My recruits were few and far between. Most

failed to excel and dropped out after a short time. Try as I might, I could never manage to land the "Big Fish"—that top-level sales performer who would catapult his lucky sponsor (me) to overnight riches.

But as I began to take charge of my own daily thought process, to interrupt my negative thoughts as they appeared and to consciously evict them from my mind, something happened. My beliefs began to change. I began to expect success. I felt more powerful even though I was not producing any better results. I felt more at peace and safe. I felt optimistic. I was having a little more fun. I was managing what I was thinking and what I was thinking was changing how I felt….both to me and how I felt to others.

Then I met Jerry Schaub.

Jerry was just another prospect that agreed to hear my presentation. Just like hundreds before.

But I felt different both to me and to this prospect…just enough different for him to see the opportunity and feel it all the way to his bones.

I went through the same sales presentation routine that I always did. But he looked down at my yellow pad of scribbles and said, "I can do this. Just show me how."And he meant it!

Jerry Schaub was a tiger. Over the next year, he recruited hundreds of people into my downline. I earned $100,000 in commissions from Jerry's sales in that one year alone. My confidence soared and I went out and found myself three or four more Jerry Schaubs in the next year.

I became a master recruiter. I wasn't using any new technique. I was selling the same opportunity I'd been selling for four years. The only thing different was my willingness to train myself to think like a successful person.

Before I began to change the way I thought I was simply projecting too much doubt. People would sense something was wrong, and then put me off. But now, my energy level matched the words I was saying. People pay much more attention to who you are than to what you're saying.

These ideas have been around for centuries. All you have to do is use them.

When I graduated from high school, I weighed 198 pounds, and I'm certain I was at least one-half inch taller than I am today at 5 foot 9 and change. The boys made fun of me in the locker room. I hated going to the beach; hadn't seen my shoelaces since I was 4. Few sports. No girls. I'd been fat my whole life.

Sometime in my mid-20s, I lost enough to weigh-in at 170-something. What a thrill! The first thing I did was run out and put my once 36-inch waist into a slim-cut pair of 32-inch Wranglers. They fit! Well, almost. My gut hung over the front, sides, and back, and I tugged at the zipper turning blue while holding my breath…but I was in! Jeans…slim cuts…cool….

I did that one for years. Too tight jeans. Too fat John.

It only occurred to me while reading a rough draft of Mach II…what was really goin' on. Those slim-cut jeans weren't a celebration of my expectation of who and how I really was—FAT!

And you know what?

I weigh 160 pounds now with pecs, triceps, and other assorted weight-lifting bumps and curves. But, unless I keep a slim, healthy, fit image of myself in front of the mirror in my mind every single day—in my head and heart—I'm fat and I'll eat, drink and behave my way into staying so.

— John Milton Fogg

VISIONS

"We hope vaguely, but dread precisely."

Paul Valery

How You See Yourself

How you see yourself is through a series of pictures, like scenes from a movie, which you visualize in your mind's eye. This movie contains vivid scenes of your expectations, of how you imagine you will perform, or of what will happen in any given situation or set of circumstances. And, you have a unique and different set of pictures for each and every conceivable kind of situation you might encounter in your life. They are all based on the decisions you have made about you.

You have literally thousands of visions. One for every situation in which you can envision yourself. You probably have a vision for:

- Your health
- Your weight
- Your body size
- Your relationship with your spouse
- Your business

When you think about these things, you see a dominant film,

you hear a dominant dialogue, and you feel a certain way about what is true and inevitable.

THESE ARE YOUR VISIONS.

Do the following exercise to see for yourself:

Take something that you want—anything that's important to you and that you truly desire. Close your eyes and visualize yourself in possession of this; already having it…already doing it…already being it. "Tune in" the movie of you in that specific situation.

Let yourself flow with it. Watch the movie. Let yourself FEEL how it would feel. LISTEN to the voices, yours and others. Hear the sound-track of your life at that moment. Do that right now. Take one minute. Stop. Check your watch…give yourself 15 seconds.

This exercise can be one of the most important moments in this book. Don't cheat yourself like I did. Do the work. Don't turn the page until you do the work. Close your eyes. In one minute, open them and answer the following questions:

• • • • • • • • • • • • •

1. On a scale of 1 to 10, was the picture you saw clear?
    (1 being a blank or snowy screen, and 10 a crystal clear, wide-screen, four-color, Dolby surround-sound movie vision.)

    (Unclear) 1 2 3 4 5 6 7 8 9 10 (Clear)

2. On a scale of 1 to 10, did you feel a sense of positive or negative expectation regarding whether that result would (not could) actually happen or not?

    (Negative) 1 2 3 4 5 6 7 8 9 10 (Positive)

3. On a scale of 1 to 10, did you feel you really deserved it?

    (No) 1 2 3 4 5 6 7 8 9 10 (Yes)

⋅⋅⋅ ★ ⋅⋅⋅

Total up your points!

24-30: There is a high probability that you are on your way. HANG ON!

20-24: Something is standing in between you and what you want. You will want to do some aggressive vision work to free this up. And, you may be making some progress.

16-20: You may want this but you really only expect for things to stay the same as they are now. You must reinvent your beliefs about this goal.

Below 16: Not only do you not believe this will happen, exactly the opposite could happen. Worry is a vision too. And, you can replace worry with a vision of success.

The decisions you have made about yourself create the picture you held in your mind throughout the last exercise. Your decisions are created by input you've received, which comes to you as conversations or experiences. This conversation originates from one, or all, of the following:

Outside input—such as what people have told you.

Experiences you've had—"the facts."

Your internal dialogue—your own conscious mind chatter.

The input you receive is just like programming a computer. Without software—the input—a computer is useless.

So, in a very real sense, we ARE our programming—our movie script.

Our minds are the most intricate, powerful computers imaginable. They're literally worth billions in what they can enable us to accomplish. Just ask Bill Gates. (His net worth at the time of this writing is more than $40 billion, give or take a couple.) This self-made billionaire has not only created a fortune producing powerful software products, it's his own mental software programs that are worth billions of dollars.

The problem with our "computer" is that we've let just about everyone we've ever met program it!

Worse yet, we let *ourselves* program it. And, we usually don't know the first thing about how to write functional programs—much less

the elegant ones that create the motivation to lead us to break through our barriers to success.

Let's look at the three kinds of software we've been using to program ourselves.

Other People's Input

Whether from our parents, relatives, friends, teachers, television, the clergy, music, books, newspapers, movies, magazines, etc., one major source of our beliefs of what's expected of us was formed by input from outside influences. And, the more respected and admired the source, the more quickly we adopted that input as "true" and believed it unquestionably.

Here are some examples of other people's input:

NEGATIVE

- Don't put all your eggs in one basket.

- You're not good enough.

- Why can't you be like _____?

- You can't do that.
- What are you...nuts?
- The economy is headed for trouble.
- It's dangerous out there. Be careful.
- Why do you keep screwing up?
- Just keep your nose to the grind stone.
- Don't get your hopes up.
- What makes you think you can do that?

POSITIVE

- We love you no matter what.
- You can do anything you set your heart and mind to.
- You are the smartest.
- You deserve nothing but the best.
- We are with you all the way.
- We are always here for you.
- Dream big. Life is worth it.
- Live life to its fullest.
- You are so beautiful.
- Everyone loves and admires you.

Experience

A second powerful source of beliefs comes from your past experiences. These are real, live testimonials—proof positive of who you are and what you are actually capable of doing. How can you argue these "facts" with such compelling evidence? There is a way to use only good and replace the bad.

Check out these examples:

NEGATIVE

- You've always had a weight problem.
- You've never earned more than $___ in your life.
- You have problems with relationships.
- Every time you've tried something new, you've failed.

POSITIVE

- You have succeeded at other things that were new for you.
- You have increased your income at times before.

- You have faced fear before and done it anyway.
- You have learned new things and excelled at them.
- You can change. You have before.

Self-Talk

The third—and potentially the most powerful influence in the creation of your beliefs—comes from the thoughts and feelings you tell yourself about your own experiences, and what you've told yourself about the input you received from other people.

For example, you recently read an article about how bad the economy in your area was and what a bleak future lay ahead for local businesses. The input you received was limited to the above subject, and you read it only once. But what did you add to it as you talked with yourself about what you thought and felt about what you had read?

Think Yourself Strong

You may not need to actually go to the gym to get the benefits of a gym workout. Just imagining yourself there may do the job. Dave Smith, a sports psychology researcher at Manchester Metropolitan University in England, gathered 18 men and had six of them contract their pinkie fingers as hard as they could for 20 minutes a day, two times a week. Six others were instructed to just imagine themselves doing the exercises. And a third control group of six did nothing at all. After 30 days, the pinkies of the first group were 33 percent stronger. Those of the control group were unchanged. But the men who had visualized themselves doing the pinkie crunches actually increased their strength by 16 percent.

—*Natural Health*, March 1999

Did you give it any additional credibility? (After all, it appeared in a respected publication, and they—whoever they are—must know more about it than you do.) Did you make the gloomy economic picture all the more vivid by imagining other negative "what if" scenarios while combining what you'd read with your own fantasies and fears?

How often did you take that original story and clarify the details, add to it, expand and enhance it in your mind, giving it greater weight, more richness and additional credibility? And, how many times did you have these conversations with yourself? Once? Three or four more times? Dozens? Hundreds? Thousands? Look to see if all that you added—and the number of times you reviewed it—did not far outweigh the true impact of that single original piece of outside input.

Another example: Can you remember a single experience you've had that's similar to the following one, which happened to me?

One time, when I was playing little league, I got hit by a pitch. It was probably a 40-mile-per-hour "slow ball," but boy, it really hurt! And I cried. And I was humiliated because my buddies saw me cry. The incident happened only once. It happened when I was in the fifth grade, but I've thought about it and relived it at least a thousand times—especially when I'm playing baseball—which oddly enough, is about as often now as when I jump out of burning buildings.

In a nuts-o kind of way, baseball scares the heck out of me now. I'm afraid of being hit by a pitch. Not because I was hit by one single pitch, once way back in fifth grade, but because I've been hit and hurt and I've cried and have been humiliated thousands of times! Do the same thing over and over a thousand times and it makes quite an impression on what you expect will happen the next time. I can't even sit on the couch and watch a ball game on television without being hit by a pitch! Now if I were wanting to pursue a career or even the hobby of baseball I would need to replace the "Hit with the Pitch" movie in my mind with one of me winning the World Series and I would need to watch it a thousand times.

The reason our "rerun" conversations and self-talk have such a powerful effect is due to one of the most profound statements we can make about the human mind. It's truly the most useful gift given to mankind.

Prove it to yourself.

Have you ever cried at a movie?

Have you ever screamed at a movie?

Have you ever laughed at a movie?

All of these moments are vividly imagined events that you, your body, your mind and your soul reacted to as though they were real.

Our mind does not distinguish between a real experience and one that we have vividly imagined!

5

YOUR MOVIE IS REAL

★ ★ ★ ★ ★

"The truth that makes men free is,
for the most part,
the truth which men prefer not to hear."

H. Agar

• • • ★ • • •

There are two basic parts of our mind. Our conscious mind which is kind of the top of our head…it provides reason and judgment and discernment. Our conscious mind CAN tell the difference between a real experience and one that has been vividly imagined. However our conscious mind compared to the rest of our mind is fairly useless in terms of accomplishing great things.

The rest of our mind…our subconscious mind, which includes our BELIEFS, our FAITH, our COURAGE, our INSPIRATION, our EMOTIONS and our CREATIVITY. That part of us has led us out of the ice age, out of a barbaric existence into the world of abundance we live in today. And it is this part of us that can accomplish anything… electric lights, airplanes, computers, the Internet, the end of the Cold War, embracing cultural diversity. Everything we ever have accomplished and everything we ever will comes from this power. Call it whatever or whomever you choose. There is no denying it is there for us to use.

How many of you saw the movie *Philadelphia?* Do you remember Tom Hanks playing the part of the lawyer that contracted AIDS? Do you remember being touched by that story? Do you remember tearing up…just a little? Do you remember maybe even trying not to get emotional but getting so anyway?

Do you also remember knowing all the while that this was just a movie? Do you remember knowing that Tom was getting well paid to act the part? Do you remember knowing that he probably did not actually die, as was shown in the movie? Has it occurred to you that perhaps he never even had the dreaded disease?

This scenario demonstrates the difference between how our conscious mind "knows" things but

those things don't really matter much. And, when the powerful parts of us are subjected to a movie that moves us...it moves us. We respond as though what was playing in our head and our heart was actually real...even if we don't want to respond...we do anyway...every time.

It's true.

A vividly imagined experience has the same programming quality and impact as an actual, "real" experience.

To the powerful part of our mind, they are the exact same thing!

You see, even a real experience is no more than a perception of your mind. You have an experience and you have a perception of that experience. Your thoughts and feelings are the vision of what that experience was for you. And, your perception is not the only true perception of that experience. Other people who witness your experience may see something entirely different—and they frequently do.

Here's the key: You MAKE UP what happened by the thoughts and feelings you have about your experience. Think for a moment of a particular event that happened to you a long time ago—something you did which was stupid or embarrassing—something you called "a failure." Now, how many times did that particular event actually happen?

Hopefully only once. But how many times have you relived that event, vividly picturing every single detail, every thought, every feeling and sensation you experienced? Twenty or thirty times? Hundreds, perhaps thousands?

Every time you relive that one event, it has the exact same impact on you as the very first time it happened—and the exact same quality.

What do you suppose happens when you multiply that quality hundreds or even thousands of times? (And remember, in the previous example it was the quality of failure.) Can you see how easy it is to live your entire life based on the expectations you formed from that one single, isolated event?

Remember my story of stealing the sunglasses from Red's Market at the age of five and how I learned that telling the truth was painful and humiliating?

How many times do you think I relived my perception of that event? What kind of mindset do you suppose that created?

All of this—the experience itself… what you've been told about it and what you told yourself about it…the thoughts and feelings… all the pictures…the movie you created from your self-talk script… and all the times you've seen it over and over again—all of this goes together to create the beliefs you have about yourself…to create the expectations you have for your future. And, the simple, stunning secret here is…

WE MAKE IT ALL UP!

Think about that…

None of it is true. The script you are working from has nothing to do with the truth. The only real truth here is that you made it all up!

Is telling the truth really more painful than lying?

Is it true that any of us are not worthy of a loving spouse?

Is it true that anything that ever happened to you once is the way you are?

Well, yes and no. What's true is that who you are and what you will accomplish with your life is a self-fulfilling prophecy. The truth is what you choose it to be, and if you do not consciously choose, you subconsciously choose.

Most of us have been asleep at the wheel our whole adult lives. Wanting successful lives and working hard for them, only to let a miffed 5-year-old determine our destiny.

We have unknowingly used this extraordinary gift to actually live a small, quiet, safe life rarely venturing out to grab our own brand of brass ring. A few things were said and a few things happened that were so empowering that we spent the next thirty years watching those movies over and over again.

We can use this gift (and I know many of you have) to turn our lives on a dime and produce more wellness, more aliveness, more fun, more joy , more love and more abundance in the next five years than in our last twenty. We can accomplish that by honoring this gift on purpose, and by design with some mastery of the process.

THE NEW
SCREENPLAY

★ ★ ★ ★ ★

"Man is made by his belief. As he believes, so he is."

Bhagavad-Gita

• • • ★ • • •

We made up all the beliefs we have about ourselves. We made something up based on what happened or what we thought happened or what someone told us happened. And then, we went about learning to believe in those stories by listening to them over and over again.

Babies don't have any beliefs. They do not believe the average person cannot earn $100,000 a year—yet most adults don't believe that's possible for them.

Babies do not believe in E=mc^2— yet most adults do.

Babies do not have a particular religious belief—yet most adults do.

Babies are not racist or sexist, capitalists or communists, republicans or democrats, successes or failures. Human beings are not born believing anything.

All we are at birth is a clean slate for limitless possibilities.

So, how do we break through to access all of our dreams and aspirations?

First…

We, give up our right to be right about us.

(You may want to read that again.)

We, give up our right to be right about us.

Most of us hold on to what we believe to be true—about life and most everything else—as if there were no possibilities for any other truth. Breaking through your barriers to success requires that you make up new ideas of what's possible, so that your possibilities support and empower your desires. It comes down to a new screenplay.

Say, for example, you currently weigh 150 pounds. You want to weigh 125, but your expectation and belief is that you weigh, and will continue to weigh, 150 pounds. How do you know what your vision is? Pay attention to what you have been doing, eating, exercising or not.

With what you've learned so far, you know you will have to create a new expectation that you weigh 125 pounds. But that expectation will fly right in the face of what you know to be true! And, any thought other than that "truth" (that you weigh 150 pounds) will immediately seem to you to be phony or stupid. Obviously, visualizing yourself weighing 125 pounds is not true. In fact, it's a lie.

Why even suggest it? In this scenario, what's possible for us appears useless at best, and at worst, a lie. In short, there is no possibility. It's impossible!

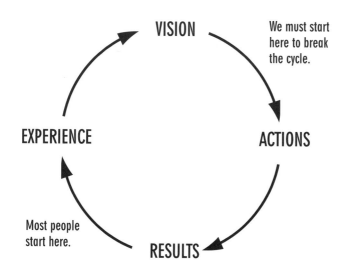

VISION

We must start here to break the cycle.

EXPERIENCE

ACTIONS

Most people start here.

RESULTS

Consider this:

The reason you do weigh 150 pounds is because you believe that's the truth! And because of that belief, you have been subtly, though powerfully, motivated—to eat just enough, laze around just enough, and justify it all just enough—to remain that way.

So, what can you do?

Give up your belief in yourself as a 150-pound person in exchange for the possibility of weighing 125 pounds. Give up your right to be right in exchange for being successful…in exchange for getting what's possible.

Creating a New Screenplay of Beliefs

Creating a new belief is like dying cloth in the old traditional way. Native Americans would

take a piece of natural fabric and change it into a different color by soaking the cloth in a dye, squeezing it out, hanging it up to dry and set, and continuing the process over and over again until the cloth ended up the color they wanted—the color they thought was possible to achieve.

At first, there was little, if any, change in the color of the fabric. It took many soakings, rinsings and settings, and the change of color was gradual. Although at times the change was hardly noticeable, the new color deepened each time. After a while, this change accelerated, becoming richer faster until soon there was no hint of the original color. The old color was gone and in its place was the new color.

Our beliefs are created the same way. This "dying" process with our beliefs occurs in the mind and is known as imprinting. We have the extraordinary ability to create thoughts at will, and we can imprint those thoughts on and into our minds at will, as often as we choose—literally hundreds of times each day! Like the depth of the color of a piece of dyed cloth, we can also control the quality and intensity (i.e., power) of the imprint we create. To the degree that our picture has clarity and detail, and can be expressed and experienced by our senses and emotions, our mind will respond to it as if it is a real experience. The richer and more complete the image, the greater its impact in and on your mind.

Just decide to change your mind. You change your mind whenever you want to. Just do it now!

In creating new beliefs and expectations, the greater the clarity and detail, the greater the quality and power of the imprint. Let's use the ever-popular weight issue as an example of creating clarity and detail. Ask yourself these questions and answer them with as much detail and specificity as you can:

- What exactly is an excellent weight for you?

- What exactly do you look like at that weight?

- What's the shape of your body at that weight?

- Describe the new lines, curves, contours and the definition of muscles you see now?

- What do you think about when you see yourself in the mirror?

- What does the scale indicate when you step on it?

- How do your clothes fit?

- What do your new clothes look like? How do you look wearing them?

- How do you feel at this new weight?

- Are you doing any new activities now? What do you like best about them?

- What are people saying to you about the new you?

- What are people saying about how good you look?

- How do you feel about that?

- Do you have any new attitudes?

- Are you more confident...more attractive...more secure...happier?

You may think that your answers to these questions sound silly, very phony or contrived. That's fine. Realize that your answers are providing a powerful clarity— your answers are filling your mind with a richness that's the equivalent of having a real life experience. In fact, because so many of us tend to sail through life, to a great degree unaware of all that's happening around us and even within us, our answers actually create a kind of "bigger and better than life" experience in our minds.

*de.cide vt. [de-, off, from + *caedere* to cut] 1. to end (a contest, dispute, etc.) by giving one side the victory or by passing judgement 2. to make up one's mind or reach a decision about; determine (to *decide* which tie to wear) 3. to cause to reach a decision.

SYN.—decide implies the bringing to an end of vacillation, doubt, dispute, etc., by making up one's mind as to an action, course, or judgement; **determine** in addition suggests that the form, character, functions, scope, etc., of something are precisely fixed (the club *decided* on a lecture series and appointed a committee to *determine* the speakers, the dates, etc.); **settle** stresses finality in a decision, often one arrived at by arbitration, and implies the termination of all doubt or controversy; to **conclude** is to decide after careful investigation or reasoning; **resolve** implies firmness of intention to carry through a decision (he *resolved* to go to bed early every night).

—Webster's New World Dictionary

7

WHO ARE YOU
TO PLAY SMALL?

★ ★ ★ ★ ★

"The reasonable man adapts himself to the conditions
that surround him...the unreasonable man
adapts surrounding conditions to himself...
all progress depends on the unreasonable man."

George Bernard Shaw

Who Are You to Play Small?

Our deepest fear is not that we are inadequate. Our deepest fear is that we are powerful beyond measure. It is our light, not our darkness, that most frightens us. We ask ourselves, "Who am I to be brilliant, talented or fabulous?" Actually, who are you not to be?

You are a child of God. Your playing small doesn't serve the world. There's nothing enlightened about shrinking so that other people won't feel insecure around you.

We are all meant to shine as children do. We were born to make manifest the glory of God that is within us. It's not just in some of us, it's in everyone. And as we let our own light shine, we inconspicuously give other people permission to do the same. As we are liberated from our own fear, our presence automatically liberates others.

—Marianne Williamson

• • • ★ • • •

Do you believe our creator would allow us to have a worthwhile desire and then not give us the ability to achieve it?

That would be mockery. It would be cruel.

Dr. Napoleon Hill proved in his lifelong study of 500 of the most successful, self-made people in America:

"What the mind of man can conceive and believe, it can achieve."

Look around the world. Look at the people who are eternally happy and peaceful. Look at the 70-year-olds who compete in marathons and the elders who are living comfortably past 100. Look at the heroes and heroines who have made such a difference in our lives through their contribu-tions. Look at our societies and world leaders. Look at the people who individually have made more money than some countries. The world is full of abundance, achievement, influence, respect, love and health. It is there for the borrow-ing. All you have to do is envision yourself with it, and it will come.

Most of us have been taught to pursue success by identifying what we want to do. We want new cars and we want to travel the world. Our tendency is to go directly for those things and the money that will provide them. And yet, our greatest point of leverage to achieve anything and everything we want is **not what we have, but who we are**. It is who we are, and who we are being in the moment, that creates the tangible results in our lives.

People who are broke or sick or friendless are so because of who they are being. What they have

done to create these results is simply an effect that follows that cause.

Your version of Mach II has to star you. The most powerful visions therefore are those that redefine who you are—envisioning a person who does deserve happiness, health and wealth. A person who attracts it like the powerful magnet he or she is.

The first three cornerstones below, as well as the examples, were provided by Carol McCall and her "Design Your Life" workshop. Thank you, Carol.

To create a vision of who you would love to become, access these four cornerstones:

I. Your authentic values are...

Simply those aspects of life that you treasure. What do you love about life? What must be in your daily life?

Examples of Values:

- Acceptance
- Honesty
- Perfection
- Appreciation
- Humor
- Pleasure
- Belonging
- Independence
- Power
- Comfort
- Integrity
- Recognition
- Communication
- Intimacy
- Relationship
- Contribution
- Joy
- Respect
- Creativity
- Love
- Safety
- Family
- Order
- Security
- Freedom
- Partnership
- Spirituality/God

- Fun
- Participation
- Trust
- Harmony
- Peace
- Work

For example, my Top Five Values are:
- Creativity
- Fun
- Integrity
- Love
- Success

Pick from these or make up your own. Spend some time now identifying some of your highest authentic values. Write them down here:

1. _____
2. _____
3. _____
4. _____

II. Gifts

Each of us has one or more natural gifts or talents that are contributions to other people. You may be in denial about yours, but just ask anyone who knows you well. I believe these gifts were awarded to us for a reason—so that we could share them with the world. And, I believe that we are our most powerful when we are sharing the special gifts that we are. Make sure your visions express you sharing your gifts.

· · · ★ · · ·

Examples of Gifts:
- Challenge
- Honesty
- Love
- Contribution
- Inspiration
- Music
- Creativity
- Integrity
- Spirituality
- Friendship
- Joy
- Strength
- Fun
- Leadership
- Success

For example, My Gifts are:
- Fun
- Creativity
- Leadership

Spend some time getting a sense of one of your gifts and write about it here:

_____

_____

_____

_____

_____

_____

_____

_____

_____

_____

_____

_____

_____

_____

**III. Life Purpose—
or The Theme of Your Life**

Your life theme is:
- Natural
- Passionate
- Joyful
- Fun
- Satisfying
- Unique to you

Each of us can discover a theme to our life. It's kind of like a song of our life, our personal purpose for being here. Life purpose is often confused with grandiose accomplishments such as ending world hunger or discovering a cure for cancer. Although these may be authentic life purposes for somebody, for most of us the theme of our lives is much simpler. For example: Raising a successful family, being a role model for the community, inspiring others to succeed—these might be authentic, powerful life purposes for many of you. Discovering and wordsmithing your life purpose is an ever-evolving project. Start now to think about it and write it into your vision.

My life purpose is to live life full out, have fun, and inspire others to do the same.

What do you feel the theme of your life at its most powerful level might be?

_____
_____
_____
_____
_____
_____

IV. Character Traits, Beliefs and Habits

Make a list of the ten most desired character traits, beliefs and habits that you will need to develop to become the person that attracts what you want.

Examples of Character Traits, Beliefs and Habits:

1. I act quickly on things I need to do.
2. I look for the positive and good in everyone.
3. I respect and take care of my body.
4. I deserve to be successful.
5. I play a little or a lot every day.

···★···

Add a few of your own…

6.

_____

_____

7.

_____

_____

8.

_____

_____

9.

_____

_____

10.

_____

_____

Add these new character traits, beliefs and habits to your new vision. Design your new screenplay just the way you see you will need to be to win; around who you are in your desired future. This will bring you more growth and more abundance in all areas of your life, more than any other single thing you can do.

AFFIRMATIONS

Affirmations are statements of specific goals phrased as facts. They are a way to simplify your vision and break it into simple one liners that can shape the way you see the world and the way you see yourself "being" in it. You may use affirmations to support your vision. Often it is easier to read a set of affirmations through-out the day instead of the actual vision. Do, however, read and visualize your vision once in the morning and once in the evening.

Here are some examples of affirmations:

I absolutely love myself.
I deserve abundance.
I deserve happiness.
I deserve health.
I am in action every day.
I am having fun.
I love supporting people.
I love giving people my full attention.

I love listening to people at a level that
   heals them.
I love vigorous exercise.
I am healthy and vital.
I am wealthy.
I have freedom.
I have lots of free time.
I am massively productive.
I get things done anyway.
I attract good fortune.
I attract whatever I need.
I am easy to be with.
People love listening to me.
People love being with me.
People follow me with ease
   and confidence.
I ooze confidence.
I am safe and secure.
I believe in me.
I believe in my goals.
I know success is inevitable.
Life is easy.
Life is fun.
Life is abundant.

Pick some of these or write your
own. Study them daily.

As you read through this list,
move past any challenge your
mind brings up to an affirmation.
That's just the old script, trying
to tell you what you're not. You
may want to read the list again.

Can you feel the power of that?

SHOOTING MACH II
STARRING YOU

"It is what you choose NOT to see
in your life that controls your life."

Lynn Andrews

· · · ★ · · ·

Seeing is Believing

Every picture tells a story and it's true that each picture is worth a thousand words.

You will want to use photo illustrations (whether you take them yourself or clip them from magazines) to create powerful images—pictures that support your vision.

Magnetic photo albums are perfect for this purpose. Clip pictures from magazines that accurately describe the possibilities as you see them in your future, and assemble them creatively on the pages of your "Vision Book."

If you want your body to look a certain way, check out fitness magazines for pictures of you as you want to be. Clip pictures of clothes you desire from fashion magazines; vacation spots you want to visit from travel magazines; the car you want; the stereo; grown-up toys; anything and everything that accurately

and artfully represents the things you desire to have, do, or be, and paste those pictures into your book. You can max out the power of these images by literally putting yourself in the picture. If there's a particular car you long for, take a camera to the dealer, select the make, model, color, etc., of the car of your choice, and have the salesperson snap a couple shots of you in the driver's seat. Paste that picture in your book.

If there's an outfit you desire that you've clipped from a magazine, cut out a picture of your head and paste it over the model's face. You can do this with a house, a muscular body, a scene from a distant land, an activity such as driving a race car, skydiving...anything.

Also, many magazines have sections devoted to up-and-comers, such as hot new names on the business scene, etc. You can easily create the words and pictures that list you as the subject of these articles. Put these in your book as well.

Make up a paycheck and write the weekly or monthly income you desire on it and paste that in. And, don't forget headlines and captions. Research has shown the headline of an advertisement and the captions under photographs are the most read and remembered elements of the ad. Make up your own positive, descriptive captions for your pictures.

Magazines are filled with powerful, positive headlines that you can cut out and use to give your Vision Book the one-two punch of both words and pictures.

Go on with this, making it richer and incorporating more specific elements that are unique to you and your own life circumstances.

The point is to add as much detail, as many rich, sensory ingredients, and as much passion, emotion and enthusiasm as possible. And again, avoid completely any mention of what you don't want.

You can dramatically increase the quantity of the imprints your mind receives—and therefore, their quality and power as well—simply by listening to your own self-talk,

Jim Carrey 3762 Ventura Blvd. Hollywood, CA 90256		246
	5-13 19 86	58·7890 1234
PAY TO THE ORDER OF Jim Carrey		$ 20,000,000.00
Twenty million dollars and ⁰⁰/₁₀₀		
MEMO	Jim Carrey	
⑈051503051⑈ 51 8757 0″		

Actor and comedian, Jim Carrey, wrote himself a check for $20 million and kept it in his wallet until he earned that amount for his performance in the movie, The Cable Guy. This kind of "Vision Work" is understandable from a guy who once said "It is better to risk starving to death then surrender. If you give up on your dreams, what's left?"

self-image, audio cassette tape. The script should be along the lines of the previous example, but, of course, it's your own, "customized" version.

Many stores that sell audio and video supplies have what's called "endless loop" cassette tapes. They're used for greeting messages on answering machines. These tapes are literally never-ending. They will continue to play as long as you've got your tape player turned on. They come in a variety of time lengths: 30 and 60 seconds, one-and-a-half- and three-minute cassettes. You can also burn your own compact disk or mp3 to accomplish the same thing.

Compose your script and read it into your tape recorder. Put on your best, most enthusiastic radio announcer's voice when you make your recording. Then play it back when you're riding in the car, doing mundane chores, working out, especially just before you go to sleep...any time and every

time you have the opportunity. Your script played over and over again will each time create a fresh, brand-new image imprint in your mind.

Remember, you create and deepen all of your beliefs by reliving those experiences over and over in your feeling mind. Listening to your self-talk tape is a powerful way to imprint and readjust the balance scales in your mind, in favor of the new self-image you now envision.

Now that you've got all of this wonderful stuff, what do you do with it?

At least twice every day—and more often if you will make the time—read your script or listen to your tape, look at your book and visualize yourself, fully, richly and completely living your vision and loving it.

Allow yourself to feel how you will feel when you are enjoying your success. The best times for doing this are when you first wake up in the morning and just before you drift off to sleep at night. That sort of waking-dreaming state is one where your mind is super-receptive to the imprinting process.

Each time you read, look or listen to any of this material, make sure you are as relaxed and comfortable as possible. Of course, you can listen while exercising or doing some repetitive or "mindless" activity, but it is best done when you're quiet, alone and relaxed.

That's when you're most open and receptive, and it's also when the feeling-awareness of your mind is clear of distractions, which allows it to be its most creative.

Here's a very important caution:

Initially, you may reject these images in your imprinting process as false or foolish, or you might make some other critical interpretation or judgment about them. DO NOT fight these reactions. When they surface, simply thank yourself for expressing that opinion and replace those criticisms with your positive visualizations. (Remember, you make it all up anyway, so why not make up things that empower you?) Just continue to go back to your visualizations no matter how many times you may be derailed by your old "judgmental" beliefs.

Just do it anyway…remember, if you don't change your vision, your old vision will still dominate. So, you are doing it anyway, just do it differently.

Any new vision can become real to you just by following the screenwriter's model, sometimes expressed in three questions:

1. What exactly is happening?

2. What exactly are people saying and how are they saying it?

3. How are you feeling?

With that captured, simply write the screenplay of your life.

1. Write a film script in exact detail.

2 Write it as though it was happening NOW.

3. Write it in the first person. "I am now experiencing this..."

4. Specifically write:

what you are doing
what others are doing
what you are saying
what others are saying
what you are feeling
what others are feeling

5. Avoid any words labeling what you don't want. Like:

Stop smoking
Lose fat
Pay off debts

6. Secure pictures that help tell the story.

As you visualize, see, hear, sense and especially feel—physically, intellectually and emotionally, as well—just the way you would as if you were actually living the experience here and now. Take at least several minutes for each different image you are visualizing. Throughout your day, whenever and wherever you can, create the opportunity to reflect on your vision. Place pictures on your mirror, by your phone, beside your bed, on the ceiling, in the car, above your television—better yet, tape it right over the television screen! Cover your world with these vivid and powerful reminders of your future.

In time, your new vision will become a habit. It will flow into, around and through your mind without you even having to think about it. How long this takes depends solely on the quality of your images and the quantity of the imprints themselves. It may take you weeks, a month, three months or a year. It will probably only take you a few days to begin to see the first positive results. Rest assured, your vision will take hold!

This method has NEVER failed anyone who has done it consistently. The imprinting process may work quickly for you or slowly for you, but if you stick with it, it will work for sure! The only way the imprinting process will not work is if you quit! If you quit, then it will start again with your old vision.

As your new vision TAKES hold, your mindset will elevate, creating that subtle, yet powerful motivation, which will positively impact all your actions and behavior. Your performance in nearly every area of your life and work will

• • • ★ • • •

change for the better! You will notice that you possess more and more Physical Energy… Enthusiasm…Confidence… Persistence…Passion…Desire… and Commitment…all of which are guaranteed to move your reality steadily and inevitably toward your possibilities.

You Will Break Through Your Barriers To Success! You Will Experience the movie *Mach II Starring You!*

Perhaps this all sounds pretty silly to you. Perhaps you're thinking it might be a fun project, but does it really work? Can it really work for someone like you? Believe me. It's not silly—and it absolutely does work, and it will work for you!

How to Make Your Film Script—Your Vision

1. Read your vision first thing in the morning and last thing at night.

2. As you read and look at your pictures, pause, close your eyes, and visualize yourself experiencing your vision.

3. Allow yourself to feel how you will feel. Simply watch your movie.

4. Do this for thirty days straight and your life will change dramatically.

THE MOVIE
OF YOUR LIFE

"Don't ask what the world needs. Find out
what makes you come alive and go do that.
Because what the world needs is
more people who have come alive."

HOWARD THURMAN

⋆

Since real experiences play in your memory like a movie, you'll want the vision you create to be just like a movie as well. Write a film script of a moment in your life when you are who you would love to be.

Your film script will include a full and complete description of the sets and props…the location and lighting for each and every scene. The script also includes dialog— all the conversations that are taking place, plus all the real-time action, and even how all the people in your movie think and feel about everything that's going on.

Two keys to creating a successful film script-imprint include making all of your dialogs present tense and positive. Your mind absorbs what you imagine literally, exactly as you imagine it. Therefore, your film script must be crafted so that all your possibilities are already achieved and in your possession right now. For example: the statement, "I will weigh 'X' pounds," only serves to confirm that you're still overweight.

Tomorrow is the only day which never comes, yet for most people that's the only place and time their accomplishments and aspirations ever exist. The best you can get from this kind of would-be, should-be dialog is to affirm that you're a fat person who wants to be thin…a failure, falling short of success.

Remember, desire alone doesn't cut it. So, make sure your imprint is always in the present tense.

Wordsmithing Your Vision

1. All phrases are positive.

2. All phrases are present tense.

3. Phrases describing you are written in the first person— I or we.

4. Clarity gives the vision power. Give the details of your vision.

5. Emotions, tone and energy provide clarity. Write about the emotions, the tone and the energy.

Another key is to keep it positive. Dialog or conversation

brings up pictures in our mind. So, immediately after our mind receives a negative message, such as "I don't smoke cigarettes anymore," what does it do? Right, there's the picture of you smoking.

Instead, create a positive image of what it's like for you to be free of smoking.

For example:
"My car, my home, my clothes and my breath smell clean and fresh. I am tasting new and fantastic flavors in all the foods I eat. I breathe fully, deeply, and every breath I take gives me increased energy and makes me more and more happy and alive! I am healthy! I am in control! I am free!"

Do you get the difference between that imprint and, "I don't smoke cigarettes anymore"? Stay away from negative images by using only positive phraseology (i.e., don't use "don't").

'Cinderella Story' Now Classic
The 1980 movie Caddyshack has become a comedy classic. No scene is more memorable than that of assistant greenskeeper, Carl Spackler, played brilliantly by actor Bill Murray, when he fantasizes about playing for The Masters championship while he swings at flowers with a hoe. The following text is spoken by Murray, as Carl the greenskeeper, verbatim from the movie:

"What an incredible Cinderella story, this unknown comes outta nowhere to lead the pack, at Augusta. He's on his final hole, he's about 455 yards away—he's gonna hit about a 2-iron I think.

"Oh he got all of that one! The crowd is standing on its feet here, the normally reserved Augusta crowd—going wild—for this young Cinderella, he's come outta nowhere, he's got about 350 yards left, he's gonna hit about a 5-iron, don't you think?

"He's got a beautiful backswing that's—oh, he got all of that one! He's gotta be pleased with that, the crowd is just on its feet here, uh—he's the Cinderella boy, uh—tears in his eyes I guess as he lines up this last shot, he's got about 195 yards left, he's got

••• ★ •••

about a—it looks like he's got about
an 8-iron.

"This crowd has gone deathly silent,
the Cinderella story, outta nowhere, a
former greenskeeper now—about to
become The Masters champion.

"It looks like a mirac...
It's in the hole!"

—Tom Clark, USA Today (April 2001)

DIRECTOR'S NOTES

IT ONLY TAKES A MOMENT TO MOTIVATE.

- Write about a small space in time when you have accomplished your goals.

- Write about a moment when you are feeling the most powerful feelings of success.

The following are some examples of visions. Study how they "create" a vision of success.

"I weigh _____ pounds and I'm loving every minute of it! I look fantastic!

It's great to fit into size ____ clothes that fit me perfectly and hang so beautifully from my trim, sculpted body.

I swim and sunbathe in the luxury of my new freedom. As I walk down the beach, people turn and say, 'Look at _____, (use your own name) what a great body!'

I love the way I look and so does everyone else!

I'm more active than ever before. I'm doing things most 20-year-olds can't do! I bike, play tennis and enjoy working out. When the aerobics teacher asks who is the most improved person in class, everybody shouts '_____ is!'

My friends say _____'s the most healthy and fit person they know. And they're right! I'm so proud of my lifestyle—and what's more, I'm proud to have turned so many people on to eating light and right, being vital and alive, fit and trim, looking and feeling terrific! People are calling me 'The Ambassador of Health.' They love me for it—and I love it, too.

I am a sterling example of health and creative power for everyone I meet!

I'm making a positive difference in so many people's lives.

Sample Vision

Life just got a lot easier.

Today good fortune and abundance is showering upon me. I now have the financial freedom and independence that I so richly deserve. And now I have the free time to enjoy it. Now I travel...to the exotic places of the world and I do so in total comfort and ease. I love the vibrancy of South America. I can hear the music and I can feel the vibes. The people here are so happy...so grateful and so loving. This place renews me! I love the Caribbean. The islands, the warm soft sand, the laid-backness of it all. And the water... a trillion gallon bath tub full of live toys. I could sleep here forever.

I can enjoy these places because I have secure wealth now. It flows and flows and flows. Tens of thousands of dollars in net income lifts me up and carries me where ever I choose to go. I love first class. I love service. I love the freedom of no limit fun.

These rich rewards come to me out of my development. My passion for my business. My passion for people and their goals. My passion for the abundance life has stored up for all of us. I am now the person others go to for love, for guidance, for coaching and for leadership. I am the go-to gal and I love it! I feel the freedom. I hear the silence of the ocean 30 ft under. I hear the rhythm of the music. I hear the laughter of friends and loved ones "being" here too. I feel the joy. I feel the safety. I feel the warmth. This is what I have always wanted and most importantly learned to expect. Fun, Freedom, Friends and Family. I am all in.

SUCCESS

"The important thing is this:
to be able to sacrifice what we are
for what we could become."

Charles Debois

$\cdots \bigstar \cdots$

In 1983, I purchased a mock-up of the cover of SUCCESS *Magazine* with my picture on the cover. I framed it and hung it on my wall and looked at it every day. My vision at that time was to be not only rich, but famous as well. I wanted something to prove to my friends and family that I really was cutting it. SUCCESS *Magazine* seemed like the perfect proof.

In March 1992, SUCCESS *Magazine* featured the Network Marketing industry's skyrocketing success as its lead story. It was the first time a mainstream publication had done so in the industry's 50-year history. Out of 10 million Network Marketers, they chose me for the cover and lead story.

Now, you may think this happened because I was the most outspoken, flamboyant, successful or famous person in the industry—not at all. Or, perhaps you think it was because I hired some public relations firm to make it happen. I didn't.

Actually, and rightfully so, SUCCESS wanted Rich DeVos, president of the $6-billion-a-year Quixtar Corporation (at that time, Amway), on the cover. He has created thousands of million-aires. He and his partner Jay Van Andle have built the number one Network Marketing organization in the world and they are *five*, (count them!) *five* times bigger than number two! SUCCESS *Magazine* thought he should be on the cover. He, however, did not return SUCCESS's phone call. You may think he did not return their call because he was too busy, or he didn't care. I don't think so. Rich DeVos did not return that call for only one reason...I had the picture of myself on that cover. He, obviously, did not.

RATE YOURSELF: The 64 Critical Management Skills

SUCCESS!

AMBITION
THE WINNER'S EDGE

POWER
WHO HAS IT,
HOW TO USE IT

MONEY
AND YOU

WHAT DRIVES
TODAY'S
ENTREPRENEURS

HOW TO GET
WHAT YOU WANT
IN LIFE

ACHIEVER
OF THE YEAR

"SUCCESS" IS A TRADEMARK OF HAL HOLDINGS CORPORATION REPRODUCED UNDER AGREEMENT BY FOTOZINES, INC.
REG. U.S. PATENT OFFICE

A mocked-up cover of SUCCESS Magazine
that I purchased at a fair in Ohio, May 1983.

The Hidden Psychology Behind Good Customer Service

SUCCESS

THE MAGAZINE FOR TODAY'S ENTREPRENEURIAL MIND

34 MASTERS OF MULTI-LEVEL MARKETING PROCLAIM:

"WE CREATE MILLIONAIRES"

Their Eager Disciples Build Overnight Empires

Lightning Growth: He Recruited Friends and Made $500 Million.

Sizzling Sales: His Oxyfresh Team Soared to Riches.

Wave of the Future: He Teaches MLM Tactics to Major Corporations.

CONQUER COMPLEX PROJECTS
Now, a New Generation of Tools and Techniques

PLUS
Ax Your Taxes: The Sharpest New Software
Attack Big Companies: Seize Their Niches

Actual March 1992 cover of SUCCESS Magazine. This issue outsold every issue in the 100-year history of the magazine....

ON INSPIRATION

I am a great believer in the power of inspiration to influence our own powerful visions. The following are some of my favorites. Reading and reflecting on their wisdom allows me to feel the way I feel when I'm starring in the movie of my life. You are encouraged to find and reflect on everything and anything that does the same for you.

—RICHARD BROOKE

• • •

If I feel depressed, I will sing.
If I feel sad, I will laugh.
If I feel ill, I will double my labor.
If I feel fear, I will plunge ahead.
If I feel poverty, I will think of wealth to come.
If I feel incompetent, I will remember past success.
If I feel insignificant, I will remember my goals.
Today I will be the master of my emotions.

—OG MANDINO
THE GREATEST SALESMAN IN THE WORLD

Every creative act involves…a new innocence of perception, liberated from the cataract of accepted belief.

—ARTHUR KOESTLER
THE SLEEPWALKERS

• • •

Be mindful of your thoughts…

Be mindful of your thoughts; your thoughts become your words.

Be mindful of your words; your words become your actions.

Be mindful of your actions; your actions become your habits.

Be mindful of your habits; your habits become your character.

Be mindful of your character; your character becomes your destiny.

—AUTHOR ANONYMOUS

··· ★ ···

This, therefore, is a faded dream of the time when I went down into the dust and noise of the eastern marketplace, and with my brain and muscles, with sweat and constant thinking, made others see my visions coming true. Those who dream by night in the dusty recesses of their minds wake in the day to find that all was vanity, but the dreamers of the day are dangerous men, for they may act their dream with open eyes, and make it possible.

—T.E. LAWRENCE,
INTRODUCTION TO SEVEN PILLARS OF
WISDOM 1922 (OXFORD EDITION)

· · ·

In this life, you get to be either right or happy.

—JERRY JAMPOLSKY

· · ·

If we don't change our direction, we are likely to end up where we are headed.

—CHINESE PROVERB

The Masters in the art of living make little distinction between their work and their play, their labor and their leisure, their minds and their bodies, their information and their recreation, their love and their religion.

They simply pursue their VISION OF EXCELLENCE at whatever they do, leaving others to decide whether they are working or playing. To them, they are always doing both!

—JAMES MITCHNER

· · ·

Amidst the glut of insignificance that engulfs us all, the temptation is understandable to stop thinking. The trouble is that unthinking persons cannot choose, but must let others choose for them. To fail to make one's own choices is to betray the freedom which is our society's greatest gift to all of us.

—STEPHEN MULLER,
PRESIDENT, JOHNS HOPKINS UNIVERSITY

The Four Agreements

I. BE IMPECCABLE WITH YOUR WORD.

Speak with integrity. Say only what you mean. Avoid using the word to speak against yourself or to gossip about others. Use the power of your word in the direction of truth and love.

2. DON'T TAKE ANYTHING PERSONALLY.

Nothing others do is because of you. What others say and do is a projection of their own reality, their own dream. When you are immune to the opinions and actions of others, you won't be the victim of needless suffering.

3. DON'T MAKE ASSUMPTIONS.

Find the courage to ask questions and to express what you really want. Communicate with others as clearly as you can to avoid misunderstandings, sadness and drama. With just this one agreement, you can completely transform your life.

4. ALWAYS DO YOUR BEST.

Your best is going to change from moment to moment. It will be different when you are healthy, as opposed to sick. Under any circumstance, simply do your best, and you will avoid self-judgment, self-abuse and regret.

— DON MIGUEL RUIZ

• • •

There are many who are living far below their possibilities because they are continually handing over their individualities to others. Do you want to be a power in the world? Then be yourself. Be true to the highest within your soul and then, allow yourself to be governed by no customs or conventionalities or arbitrary man-made rules that are not founded on principle.

—RALPH WALDO TRINE

How Did You Live Your Dash?

I read of a man who stood to speak at the funeral of a friend.

He referred to the dates on her tombstone; her life from beginning to end.
(1934-1998)

He noted that first came her date of birth and spoke the ending date with
tears, but he said what mattered most of all was the dash between those years.

For that dash represents all the time that she spent alive on earth....
And now, only those who loved her know what that little line is worth.

For it matters not how much we own; the cars...the house...the cash,
what matters is how we live and love and how we spend our dash.

So think about this long and hard...are there things you'd like to change?
For you never know how much time is left, that can still be rearranged.

If we could just slow down enough to consider what's true and real,
and always try to understand the way other people feel.

And be less quick to anger, and show appreciation more,
and love the people in our lives like we've never loved before.

If we treat each other with respect, and more often wear a smile...
Remembering that this special dash might only last a little while.

So, when your eulogy's being read, your life's actions to rehash...
Would you be proud of what they'll say about how you spent your dash?

—AUTHOR ANONYMOUS

••• ★ •••

A midlife crisis is when you've reached the top rung of your ladder only to realize that you've leaned it against the wrong wall.

—AUTHOR ANONYMOUS

• • •

It is not because things are difficult that we do not dare, it is because we do not dare that things are difficult.

—SENECA

• • •

People stumble over the truth from time to time, but most pick themselves up and hurry off as though nothing happened....

—AUTHOR ANONYMOUS

• • •

When one door closes another door opens; but we so often look so long and so regretfully upon the closed door, that we do not see the ones which open for us.

—ALEXANDER GRAHAM BELL

A pessimist sees the difficulty in every opportunity. An optimist sees the opportunity in every difficulty.

—WINSTON CHURCHILL

• • •

The Invitation...

It doesn't interest me what you do for a living.

I want to know what you ache for, and if you dare to dream of meeting your heart's longing.

It doesn't interest me how old you are. I want to know if you will risk looking like a fool for love, for your dreams, for the adventure of being alive.

It doesn't interest me what planets are squaring your moon. I want to know if you have touched the center of your own sorrow, if you have been opened by life's betrayals, or have become shriveled and closed from fear of

further pain. I want to know if you can sit with pain, mine or your own, without moving to hide it or fake it or fix it.

I want to know if you can be with joy, mine or your own, if you can dance with wildness and let ecstasy fill you to the tips of your fingers and toes without cautioning us to be careful, be realistic, or to remember the limitations of being human.

It doesn't interest me if the story you're telling me is true. I want to know if you can disappoint another to be true to yourself, if you can bear the accusation of betrayal, and not betray your own soul.

I want to know if you can see beauty even if it's not pretty every day, and if you can well-spring your life from a sacred presence.

I want to know if you can live with failure, yours and mine, and still stand on the edge of a lake and shout to the silver of the full moon...YES!

It doesn't interest me to know where you live or how much money you have. I want to know if you can get up after the night of grief and despair; weary and bruised to the bone, and do what needs to be done for the children.

It doesn't interest me who you know, or how you came to be here. I want to know if you will stand in the center of the fire with me and not shrink back.

It doesn't interest me where, or with whom, you have studied. I want to know what sustains you from the inside, when all else falls away. I want to know if you can be alone with yourself, and if you truly like the company you keep in the empty moments....

—ORIAH MOUNTAIN DREAMER

ACKNOWLEDGMENTS

John Milton Fogg
jmf@greatestnetworker.com

Thank you, John and Susan, for your friendship, your courage, your coaching, prodding and general badgering to get this book done. And most of all, for what you have done to bring Network Marketing the right way, along at Mach II.

Carol McCall
The World Institute Group of Companies
(800) 999-9551
www.listeningprofitsu.com

Thank you, Carol, for your infinite wisdom—in unwinding those silly things I made up that kept me from writing this book…and for your love.

My parents
Lee Brooke Combs, Johnny Combs,
Dick Brooke and Penny Brooke

Thank you for doing the many things I remember, and the many I don't, that gave me the foundation to pull this all off…and for always being there no matter what.

ALSO BY BROOKE

Mailbox Money is Richard Brooke's essential guide to Network Marketing. This inspiring book takes a look at seven, true-life, rags-to-riches stories from some of the top names in the industry. Mailbox Money presents industry facts, while dispelling many Network Marketing myths. It will provide you with a thorough understanding of Network Marketing: one of the most innovative, yet misunderstood business concepts in the world.

ABOUT THE AUTHOR

Richard Bliss Brooke, President of Oxyfresh Worldwide, Inc., and founder of High Performance People, L.L.C., has been leading, coaching and training leaders—from high school sophomores to multimillionaire business builders—for over 20 years.

Richard conducts a variety of personal and leadership development workshops and retreats. Through Richard's influence, hundreds of "new leaders" have discovered new distinctions in listening, leadership, courage, relationships, public speaking, team spirit and **big-time fun.**

In addition to *Mach II Starring You,* Richard authored the book *Mailbox Money, The Promise of Network Marketing.* He also co-authored *The New Entrepreneurs...Business Visionaries for the 21st Century.*

Richard continues to play full out from his home on the lake in the resort community of Coeur d' Alene, Idaho and a horse ranch in the

California foothills. He enjoys Harleys, golf, water sports, scuba diving, skiing, snowmobiling, helicopter flying, a good game of poker and a real Cuban cigar.

You can reach Richard at (888) 665-8484 or RB@Mach2.org.

1992

The March issue of SUCCESS Magazine features Richard and Oxyfresh on its cover. SUCCESS calls the company "Millionaire Makers".

1993

Sterling and Stone Publishing asks Richard to co author The New Entrepreneurs: Business Visionaries for the 21st Century.

1994

Richard is nominated Inc. Magazine's Entrepreneur of the Year.

1996

Working At Home Magazine co-features Richard on their cover about how to get rich working from home.

1998

Richard is inducted into the Network Marketing Hall of Fame.

1999

Network Marketing Rags to Riches is published

2000

Mach II With Your Hair On Fire is published.

2001-2002

Richard receives the Distributor's Choice Award Top-Five Trainers.

2003

Mailbox Money: The Promise of Network Marketing is published.

Where would YOU play...

If the world were your playground?

What if you could take your dreams and turn them into roaring fires of accomplishment?

Richard Brooke's Personal Vision and Self-Motivation Workshop will show you how...

for the rest of your life.

1-Day Workshop
$175 per person
(minimum 100)

3-Day Workshop
$400 per person
(minimum 75)

7-Day Retreat
$3,000 per person
(includes room & board;
minimum 8, maximum 12)

For more information on attending or hosting a life-changing seminar, please call 888.665.8484

"What you want doesn't matter, you get what you expect. Designing your Visions around who you are in your desired future will bring you more growth and abundance in all areas of your life."

—Richard Brooke

"This truly life-changing weekend was nothing I had expected, and yet everything I had hoped for. I anticipated another high-energy, on-your-feet, loud music, at-the-top-of-your-lungs kind of gathering. Instead, I got a deeply moving, introspective event that will change my life and resonate in my heart and soul for many years to come."

—Kevin Craig, Colorado

"I can sincerely say that you have changed my way of thinking more than anyone. I will always be grateful to you for making me a better person."

**— Gayle Sayers
NFL Hall of Fame Running Back**

"Richard Brooke's three-day workshop was incredible and unbelievably life-changing! The impact of what I learned is still expanding within me. I tell people that Richard is a man of few words, many questions and tremendous insight. We have never had such a powerful leader as Richard Brooke."

—Dorothy Hutson, Arkansas

"Richard's total, selfless dedication to supporting, guiding and helping us was very moving. I have never attended a retreat where I felt simultaneously so challenged and supported. I've spent my life pursuing personal development, alone and in groups, and I've never felt so completely transformed. All of my self-imposed blockages are either gone or conquerable both personally and professionally. I will never be the same!"

—Bob Fahey, Florida

We would love to read about your successes with your vision work. Please forward them to:

**Richard Brooke
High Performance People, L.L.C.
1875 North Lakewood Drive
Coeur d'Alene, ID 83814
Phone: (888) 665-8484
Fax: (888) 665-8485
E-mail: RB@Mach2.org**

To subscribe to our monthly E-zine of *Vision and Self-Motivation* e-mail us at RB@Mach2.org.

NOTES

NOTES

NOTES

NOTES

NOTES

NOTES

NOTES